I CAN STILL HEAR THEIR CRIES

E. Everett McFall

EVEN IN MY SLEEP

A Journey Into PTSD

Outskirts Press, Inc.
Denver, Colorado

I Can Still Hear Their Cries, Even In My Sleep
A Journey Into PTSD
All Rights Reserved
Copyright © 2007 E. Everett McFall
V 3.0

Cover Image © 2007 JupiterImages Corporation
All Rights Reserved. Used With Permission.

Outskirts Press
http://www.outskirtspress.com

ISBN-13: 978-1-4327-0457-5

Library of Congress Control Number: 2007923734

Outskirts Press and the "OP" logo are trademarks belonging to
Outskirts Press, Inc.

Printed in the United States of America

Dedications

By your Grace, Oh Lord, I receive assistance and inspiration. At your pleasure I am blessed beyond measure. As a traveler and a survivor of this life, I am a living testimony to your greatness. Only by your tender mercy Lord, am I still here. I thank you, Lord. Prayerfully hoping that these words are blessed and accepted, I therefore humbly dedicate this body of words to The Only One to whom all praises are due.

I also dedicate this work to the 58,196 men and women, my brothers and sisters killed in action within The Republic of Vietnam, a desolate island of war. Their deaths insured that others might live in peace, therefore I salute them. May their souls find ETERNAL PEACE...

I pray that these words also HONOR Their Lives, Their COURAGE and Their ULTIMATE SACRIFICE...

All Gave Some, THEY GAVE ALL...

Therefore, to all the veterans that have served this country honorably, I humbly say:

"Mission Accomplished, Job Well Done, and Welcome Home— **Welcome Home.**"

Acknowledgements

To My Precious Wife Jessica—

Dear heart, you make this journey enjoyable and worthwhile. "My Precious Sweet Kitten," I am grateful for your genuine giving nature (the spirit within you), your sincere kindness, your gentle warmth, and so much more... thanks for all that you do. I appreciate your tenderness, acceptance, your tolerance, and most of all for loving me. It is the Creator that gives life; it is the Creator that sustains life. It is the Creator to whom all life must return. The Master Designer has blessed me with the greatest gift ever—your LOVE.

—Your Hus'band

To my Father Cornelius McFall, you've made my world a better place "Dah Dah." I love you and deeply treasure you Daddy.

To my "Mom" and "Pop," Ida and Hubert Jackson, I could never love you or thank you enough for your compassion, love, and my big Brother and Sister (James and Betty).

To my family, I value you, I love you, and I praise your patience as I seek your understanding.

To the Medical and Psychiatric staff members of the Veterans Administration Health facilities nationwide, especially the

Jessie Brown VA Medical Center in Chicago, IL- PTSD Clinic. Thank you for identifying, illuminating and treating the source of my torment and pain.

To Minister Kylynn Brown and Mary C. Nolan, my editors, your skill and literary expertise produced a professionally crafted, ready for print book.

To Dr. Regina Jones, without your valuable advice and guidance, my poetic compilation would still be just a raw manuscript.

To my loving "Brother," Jay E. Keck, his family, and all of my other fellow Veterans who returned–"Welcome Home." To those who **haven't** as of yet found their way back home…I pray for your souls.

To each and every person who listened, clothed, fed, gave me shelter, financial assistance, and comfort when I was homeless and in need…May God Bless You All with the very best of Health, Happiness, Prosperity, and Love.

Foreword

E. Everett McFall has produced a moving testament to the enduring pain that stems from the horror of war. A sensitive, intelligent person whom I first met when he was a student in my Vietnam War course, he has written in a style that is raw, searing and ruthlessly honest. His journey to come to grips with what he encountered in Southeast Asia has been a long but successful one, and his poetic memoir should help other veterans and be an inspiration to all who read it. *THIS IS A MUST READ*!

Dr. James B. Lane PhD is a Distinguished Historian and Author who has written over thirty-five publications during his tenure as a Professor of History at Indiana University Northwest.

A Long time ago in a land far away, I went to war for LBJ. Nearly three million of us served in that country Vietnam. We returned with a lot of broken parts and Purple Hearts. For those who have not seen, No explanation is possible. For those who have seen, No explanation is necessary.

I'm very proud of "Doc" McFall; he was able to reveal with plain, graphic words, 'combat conditions,' as they were. He has laid it out for even nonmilitary folk to understand, especially for those not touched by the Vietnam War. More importantly, he provides an insight into the plight of those of us who suffer from PTSD. Thank you my Brother for sharing your story, the misery of war as well as its aftermath—the mental hardship of death and destruction, the nightmares and flashbacks with vivid intrusive and suicidal thoughts. You opened up your soul, exposing your human feelings, the agony of postwar psychological trauma. We pray for you, your recovery, your loving and caring wife Jessica, and your renewed relationship with God ("Big Ernie", to us 'Nam Vets').

E. Everett is a survivor who keeps on keeping on, a Marine who does not know the how to give up. "I Can Still Hear Their Cries, Even in My Sleep" is a *Journey out of the Darkness of Hell into the Light of Hope and Recovery.* It's also a *Journey of Possibility and Healing from the Horrors of War, to God's Victory and Peace of Mind.*

"Doc McFall," *YOUR BOOK IS A MUST READ FOR ALL!* Keep on writing, my Brother! Keep the Faith, just let the past go, and let God handle it! In the end, "Heaven Will Bless."

Welcome Home...

Semper Fi
Pfc. Jay E. Keck, Machine Gunner
Vietnam Veteran Class of 1966-67
Echo 2/7 1st Marine Division
Aka: www.vietnambogeyman.com

"Medic—Corpsman UP"

Contents

---

*   Denotes poems by Pfc. Jay E. Keck, USMC
**   Excerpts and passages from:
         "Dancing With Death - All Gave Some, Some Gave All"
         © 2005 E. "Doc" Everett McFall

Introduction Narrative

As a mere somewhat naive youth, I was embarking on an age-old ritual, apparently genetically embodied within the 'rites of manhood.' This passage from "baby-to boy-to man" formed a journey of apprentice warriors who sought the highest level of self-esteem, approval, acceptance, and the acknowledgement as a "MAN" from within his Society. The facts of the business were, some folk, myself included, believed that a man ain't a real man until he's been tested under fire in combat.

I answered this nation's call to arms with a vow and a fervent conviction to overcome all obstacles, defeat any adversaries, and maintain the highest level of courage, pride, and honor enjoyed by the brave men and women of uncommon valor. These heroes and sheroes who have always served this country with merit, have defended our flag, our rights, and our philosophy of life with blood, sweat, and tears, and their last breath. As a member of The Armed Forces of the United States of America, I took my oath seriously and pledged to be rigid, steadfast, bold, relentless, and determined to persevere, emerging VICTORIOUS. I went off to war as a young eager volunteer, just one of millions who would honorably serve in America's longest war ever.

Awestruck, nervous anticipation, conflicting weird and wonderful feelings flowed through this youthful U.S. Marine Medical Corpsman from Chicago, IL. On November 10th 1966, I first surveyed and inhaled this ancient oriental country bordered by China to the north; Laos and Cambodia on its west. Vietnam is a narrow elongated country with a coastline that extends its entire length. A country that foreign invaders and occupiers ruthlessly dominated and controlled during most of its four thousand year history, and most of that time it was plagued by war. Its people were proud, yet mostly poor peasants, who sought only for autonomy and the right to self-determination with total religious freedom. (Didn't the colonial Americans fight for those very same reasons?) Vietnam's lush valleys and hills flowed with the wind. This Southeast Asian tropical country was extremely "Hot" even with a high rate of rainfall, which enhanced its breathtaking natural beauty. Those steep rugged mountains coupled with that searing blistering heat, the tropical jungles, and vast tracks of wet marshlands, bordered by that ever-present rusty red colored soil (thick muddy slush after a rainfall), was the perfect backdrop for a war.

"I have PTSD, Post Traumatic Stress Disorder. It's an instant video play-back in my mind, with cranial surround sound. I am also a recovering functional alcoholic and drug abuser. I have been reliving and revisiting my tour in Vietnam, daily since 1967." A Veterans Administration psychotherapist at the Jessie Brown VA Hospital in Chicago, IL, instructed me to write down my thoughts, concerns, and fears. I was told to express my feelings as openly and clearly as possible, without reservation. I penned a two page statement that identified the "triggering" elements of my 'flashbacks' and 'nightmares'. That statement evolved into chapters of memories. From those memories this book of poems was born. That pain-staking process has started the process to free my mind and hopefully, the poems in this book will enlighten yours.

E. Everett McFall, USMC Hospital "Corpsman"
Vietnam Veteran - Purple Heart Recipient

You Forgot, I Can't

For you it was the nightly news,
For us it was raw reality.

You called for pizzas and soda,
We called for air support.

You watched construction,
I preformed destruction.

You watched children play,
I watched them die.

You learned about life,
I learned about death.

Your passion was to succeed,
Mine was to survive.

You served dinner,
I served my country.

You Forgot,   NOW   I Can't!!!

Author Unknown

Remember,

It was the Veteran, not the reporter,
who has given us freedom of the press.

It was the Veteran, not the poet,
who has given us freedom of speech.

It was the Veteran, not the lawyer,
who has given us the right to fair trial.

It was the Veteran, not the campus organizer,
who has given us freedom to demonstrate.

It was the Veteran, who salutes the flag,
who served under the flag.

and whose coffin is draped by the flag,
who allows the protester to burn the flag.

Author Unknown

I never knew that my grandmother, Margie Holiday-Love, was gravely ill. Knowing that I wouldn't be able to fully concentrate on my combat duties had I known just how sick she was, my family decided not to tell me of her terminal illness or her surgery. During her last days in this dimension, she repetitively asked, "Is Ernest coming home?" and, "When is Ernest coming?" My mother and grandmother are gone; I wasn't there for them when they passed. Dear God, Please forgive all of their sins and enter them into Paradise.

Momma and Big Momma
(Helen and Margie)

Dear Big Momma, When You Needed Me
I Wasn't There For You,
Dear Momma, When You Needed Me
I Missed Your Passing Too!

Watching the Same Stars across the Sea
Yet, I Wasn't There For You.
Lady Day, Mother, who gave birth to me
I Wasn't There For You.

You and Big Momma Are Gone
Please Lift the Burden of Pain
Loneliness and Guilt My Song
I Hear You Call My Name.

Echoes of Your Voices, Linger it's True
Shadows of Memories of Both of You
Dear Momma and Big Momma,
I'm Sorry I Wasn't There for You.

They had taught me that the journey of life would not be an easy road to travel, and there would always be challenges to overcome. Thanks for making me strong.

SIDE BY SIDE
by Pfc. Jay E. Keck, USMC

Side by side we fought and died,
One by one we came home to hide.

Side by side for 12 or 13 months,
They didn't call us soldiers. They called us grunts.

Side by side, and day by day,
Our squad leaders trying to show us the way.

Side by side the black, brown, reds, and whites,
Risking our lives in firefights.

Side by side, mostly young men,
Fighting a war we thought we could win.

Side by side, in the jungles and mountains,
The rivers and streams became our drinking fountains.

Side by side, in rice paddies and plateaus,
In a far away country we did not know.

Side by side we went to war,
To stop the communists on a foreign shore.

Side by side, trying to keep our buddies alive,
Everyday and night it took all our training to survive.

Side by side we laughed and cried,
So many being wounded, so many that died.

Side by side we fought for our flag,
Many of our friends returned in a body bag.

Side by side we fought for what was right,
Coming home to America was such a fright.

Side by side we are forever more,
Never to be forgotten by the Vietnam War.

Little Tiny Faces

I see little tiny faces
Hands stretched out and up
Ravaged by a life of War
Potbellied barefoot children
Seeking, Pleading, Wanting, Begging, and Needing.

I see little tiny faces
Hands stretched out and up
Ravaged by the plight of War
Some silently crying and withdrawn
Others Brash, Bold, Vocal, Very Animated.

I see little tiny faces
Hands stretched out and up
Ravaged by the sights of War
Fixed stares prayerfully looking for love
Peace, Hope, Happiness, Resolution or Solution.

I see widows and orphans
Little Tiny Faces
Their eyes Reveal, Glazed eyes Conceal
Expectation, Humiliation, Anticipation, Desperation
A Mirrored Reflection, and Hopeless Rejection Etched
On those Little Tiny Faces.

What is a Marine?

Neither Mammal, Fowl nor Animal
This Marine floats on Water,
Fights on Land and in the Air.
A Leatherneck as he's known too
From his first uniform stiff and blue.
A Warrior Willing to Give More
In Defense of Freedom, Espirit de Corps.
Adapt, Improvise and Overcome
Whatever it Takes to get it Done.
Highly Effective, Skilled and Motivated
Trained to Kill, Destroy or Terminate.
Courage, Valor, Strength and Hope
The Eagle, Globe, Anchor, and Rope.
I'm your Son, Husband, Next of Kin
Your Neighbor, Lover, Best of Friends.
"God, Corps, Country" our Cry
Duty, Honor, Semper Fi–How High?
Yours is Not to Reason Why
Yours is only to Kill or Die.
Worldwide the First on the Scene
I'm Proud to Wear the Title of
A United States MARINE.

Heavenly Star

Let all you do to others; be as gentle as a dove,
Stand firm in your faith, be valiant and strong.
Let all you do to others; be done in pure love,
Stand firm in your faith, be vigilant do no wrong.
What you think, you do; what you do, you are,
Let what you are, shine like a Heavenly Star.

"Grunt"

Spit-shined high-top polished boots/shoes
Recite verbatim the 'general orders,' (rules).
I'm a squared away grunt set to deploy
Trained for deadly missions without joy.
We adapt, improvise, and overcome
Any obstacle, to get the job done.
Through sand, jungles, and mountain terrain
We grunt and endure, as we were so named.
Whether in the air, on land or at sea
We won't stop fighting without a victory.
Always the first warriors on the scene,
The Brotherhood of United States Marines.

USMC=Uncle Sam's Misguided Children.
       Now Grunt, "Ooorah"

Brotherhood

The "Dap," a Hug and a Shake
The 4-1-1 on Family and the 'Hood'
For you, whatever it Takes
Brother To Brother, All Good.
I Sleep, You Watch
We Depend on Each Other
You Sleep, I Watch
In Darkness undercover.
We Laughed, We Cried
Alone and Together
We Moaned, We Sighed
About "Charlie" & the Weather.
Your Life, My Life, Ours
We Depend on Each Other
Together We Count the Hours
Yes, You Are My Brother.
Apple, Delta, Chi, or the Bay
United Brotherhood Unseen Before
Strangers Once, Friends Today
Caring and Sharing, Engaged in WAR.
Here WE Are, Guns in Hand
Foreigners from the "World"
Fighting Little People in their LAND
Thoughts of MOM & a Special Girl.
Yes, I Am Your Brother
We Depend On Each Other
DAP On BROTHER BLOOD.

(The Dap—was a greeting ritual!)

Patrol on Ambush

Rain Rain has Fell, Hot Hot from Hell
Dark Dark this Night, Quiet Quiet till Light
Lay Lay in Place, Sit Sit in Waste
Tick Tick Slap Not, Leach Leach Blood Clot
Alert Alert Eyes Open, Wait Wait Peace Broken
Listen Listen Slightest Sound, Ever Ready Fire a Round
Rain Rain Watered Trail, Patrol on Ambush
In Combat Hell…"HUSH," Patrol on Ambush.

"Flashback"

I Relive Experiences, under Heavy Mortar Attack.
I heard the distant 'thump' 'thump' sounds,
Of Mortar rockets leaving their Tubes.
As those incoming rounds approached,
Truly an *Unforgettable Whistling Sound*,
Echoing and *Reverberating* the Stillness of the *Night*.
Each round whistled its *High-Pitched Song* of *Death*
Penetrating and illuminating the blackness of the night.
I wondered which one would take my last Breath?
As each incoming round announced its Arrival,
Our training kicked in, it's time for Survival.
The 'Attack Siren' wails, "*INCOMING*" "*INCOMING*" is repeated
Men scurry, barking orders on the run.
Brave anguished faces displaying raw horror.
Exploding shells, hot chunks of metal Hurling
Constant concussions, decibels deafening.
A Grayish-White cloudy smoke fills the Air,
Sparks and embers dance as fires flare.
I hear Screams "Doc over here," "I'm Hit,"
No time for agony, or doubt, "Move Out."
I wished I was invisible, but they just kept on
Whistling & Exploding, *Whistling & Exploding*.
"Incoming," coming in.

Purple Heart

They gave me this Purple Heart
For getting wounded in battle.
This purple cloth and metal device
A token, distinctive badge of honor.

Its lavish ribbon with white trim
Represents a combative injury.
To only the wounded it is given
Symbolic, the dead posthumously.

The pain is gone, wounds long healed
Leaving scars one can plainly see.
Except for the nightmares and flashbacks
Painful recall etched in my memory.

Time has sealed, often never revealed
What the mind concealed against its will.
Sudden frights, sleepless nights
Vivid sights, sounds and flashing lights

Vacant stare, blood chilling glare,
Emotions flare, then relationships tear.
Constant anxiety, lack of sobriety
Prevents this society from accepting me.

This Purple Heart worn on my chest,
Is for those wounds below my knee.
They are all evident and plain to see,
Except the scars in my mind called PTSD.

The Ooorah Warrior

The Things we See and Smell
  Hear, Taste, Think and Do,
    So Shocking you'll never Tell
    Under Normal Skies Blue.
      Sights not Seen by Amber Eyes
        Horrible Deeds Done to Survive.
          I Hate this War and the Warrior
            That I've Become, Help Me, Creator.

              Earthy Moisture Steaming Raw
              Pungent Gagging Awful Stench
            Decaying Soil, Fresh Yesterday
          Thick Odors Far and Near
        Death, Sweat, Fungus and Fear.
      Decaying Flesh, Human and Others
    From Air, Earth, Water and Us
  Foul Bowel, That's Human Guts.
Honor the Warrior not the War
  Proud to Serve, What are we Fighting For?
    Pain of Pain, Valley of Disdain
      Guilt Sorrow, Hopelessness and Fear
        Black Cloak of Death Be Still
          Prey Not My Life, Me Pray Again.
          The Ooorah Warrior is Here
            As your Agent and by Your Will
              Traveling once More in the Valley,
                The Enemy I must KILL…

Easy Bake Oven with You Inside
Intense Heat You Sweat Your Pride.
Beyond the Hazy Morning Mist
A Distant Bright Tiny Light,
Pulsating flickering never Fading
Always Bright Tiny White Light.
An Ache, a gnaw, a Tug in the Gut
Flashing Life's Memories Treasure
So Colorful So Detail, Joyous Pain
Oh but Just, to Relive Them But
Just Once more Again;
The Tales Retold, A Better End.
Too Late NOW, In the Light I Bathe
Faint low Volume Voices Echo Sound.
Swirling Twirling Wind Cold and Warm
Time Wasted Unrewarded DEEDS,
Glory, Shame, Rejoice the Farmers' Seed,
The Flute, The Piper Vibrates His Reed.

Pain of Pain, Valley of Disdain
Tis 'My Sweet Chariot,' like
The Hum of a Single Drum
Thu-rump, thu-rump Dum Dum
Listen to 1,000 Voices
Sing Low, Sing Slow
Oh Yes, for Now I Know
For Whom the Bells Toll…
I STILL HEAR the Whistling Sounds
"INCOMING"
"Doc, Doc Wake UP,
It's Time to "Rock and Roll."

"OOORAH!!!"

The Eyes of Death

You Never Forget the Eyes,
The death rattling sounds,
Your mind seeks to drown
The labored breathing and vacant lifeless eyes
Life loss, You despise.

The decaying smells of death and the dying,
You never forget the eyes.
Vivid flashbacks without trying,
Still, you'll always remember,
The Haunting Eyes of Death

Undying Memories

I've spent my entire adult life
    Remembering, trying to forget 364 days.
I've spent countless days, sleepless nights
    Reliving, wishing they never existed.
I've spent a lifetime with segmented visions of memory
    Recalling death and life in vivid color images.
I've spent an eternity with bloodshot eyes then and now
    Pondering the value of life itself, and its cost.
Shall I spend forever as an indentured servant of insanity,
    Combating the sources of dread,
Caught in the horror of humanity, visited by the Dead?

Rape

Will you feed me?
Will you kill me?
Will you feed me?
Will you rape me?
Again and Again

GI, you give
GI, you take
GI, you rape
GI, you help me
Please, oh please

You rape my country
You rape my family
You rape my life
You rape my home
You rape my mind
Over and Over and Over
You RAPED Me

Death Angel

A tiny Sparrow that once Soared in the sky,
Lay Lifeless on earth for reasons I know not why.
This Majestic Creation once Pulsated, Alive
Now a Shell, Stilled, took its Final Dive.
Farewell, we'll meet Again
SLEEP Now! REST IN PEACE

JUST JOHN

John Walked, a strange Sight
John Leaned, slightly to his Right.
John Laughed, no matter What
John Belched, and Held his Gut.
John Stuttered, Softly as he Spoke
John Sighed, when he told a Joke.
John Prayed, for mankind's Peace
John Watched, as others Slept.
John Loved, Lived for Him on High
John IS DEAD, WHY? DEAR GOD WHY?

O' Soul

O Soul within my Mind
O Soul infinite Devine
O Soul who Guides me
O Soul I bow down to Thee

O Soul giver and Sustain
O Soul your words Reign
O Soul urge; show, Instill
O Soul living by Your Will

O Soul to obey we Strive
O Soul Creator on High
Alpha and Omega Praise I Make,
To You O Soul as I Prostrate.

A Trigger

I still hear the whistling sounds
of incoming mortars in my mind,
the echoes of WAR, my constant reality.
PTSD is an unforgiving escort,
yielding nothing positive,
lingering endlessly,
casting dark shadows of doubt
on my own sanity.

From: Jay E. Keck's, "Poems from the Bogeyman"

Everyone has a Bogeyman, (that thing of fear) that pops up when you least expect it or want it. The Bogeyman is never far away. Just as a butterfly goes through a metamorphosis, from something that crawls and is not always so pretty, into a thing of beauty and flight, we also evolve, as we face the things we fear most in life. It will bring growth, change, and most importantly, *healing*.

Vietnam Bogeyman
by Pfc. Jay E. Keck, USMC

The Vietnam Bogeyman is in my head
He'll probably be there until I'm dead.
The Vietnam Bogeyman followed me home
He goes with me wherever I roam.
The Vietnam Bogeyman is in my home
He walks the floors, he roams and roams.
The Vietnam Bogeyman eats with me
He's in my john when I go to pee.
The Vietnam Bogeyman won't let me be
He's on every station when I watch TV.

The Vietnam Bogeyman is always around
He even goes with me when I leave town.
The Vietnam Bogeyman is in my bed
Maybe that's why it's the nights I dread
The Vietnam Bogeyman is in my chair
He's even with me when I comb my hair.
The Vietnam Bogeyman is on the radio
This is a fact. This I know!
The Vietnam Bogeyman goes with me fishing
I wish he'd go away. This I am wishing.

The Vietnam Bogeyman is there when I get dressed
I wish he'd die, and (then my world) would be blessed.
The Vietnam Bogeyman is in my shower
He's right beside me every hour.
The Vietnam Bogeyman is in my dreams
If my wife wasn't with me, I'd surely scream.
The Vietnam Bogeyman I see in the rain
Why does this animal cause so much pain?
The Vietnam Bogeyman is behind every door
I wish I could crush him on the floor.

The Vietnam Bogeyman is alive and well
He followed me home, from a place called Hell.

Have you seen your Bogeyman (today)?

Tic Tic Tic

Memories are poisonous acids
Laying dormant deep within
Without rhyme nor reason, it's
Unselective torment to my brain.

I cry when emotions soar
I argue then tempers flair
I debate with confrontation
I challenge, I'm never wrong.

Firmly against blatant humiliation,
I will pursue personal retaliation.
Your retreat, the best solution,
For our peace and an amicable resolution.

Or prepare to battle with sudden rage,
Engage to the death, so mote it be.
Warning! Please don't tread on me,
Caution! Short Fuse—Combat Veteran
Internal Time Bomb Ticking...P.T.S.D.

The Art of the Kill

Part 1
I Touch my Bill, Hush be Still
Here I Fulfill, my country's Will
Aim with Skill, Now I Kill.

By chance you Engage, Display your inner Rage
Aim with Skill, Shoot to Kill
Report body Count, before you Dismount.

Hamlet or City, Ravage or Pity
Aim with Skill, Die or Kill
Forced or Willing, the Coldness of Killing.

Touch my bill, Silence be Still
Aim with Skill, Freeze; breathe, Kill
If you do me—It's Voodoo, If I do you—It's Boo boo!

Part 2
I Taste my Disdain, I feel your Pain
I See your Eyes, I hear your Cries
Speak to my Humanity, Stop this Insanity

At them aim at Will, Enjoy blood Spill
Forgive me Lord, Animal instinct, Void
Of one Accord, Me—my Enemy

Sharing a Destiny, Living to Defend
One tragic Moment, when No one Wins.
Eyes enlarged—Gazed, Shadowy death, Hazed.

Part 3
Living for the Hunt, a Passion, a Rush, a Thrill
Heart Pounding, You climb an Emotional Hill
Parched Lips, Nervousness—tingling Fingertips

Target in Sight, Trigger pull so slight
Zapped! I Watch Your Exploding Flesh,
The Anticipation yields Feverish Exhilaration

Internal consultation, Better You Than Me.
Your Spirit Abused, Your Candle Defused
The Earth, Eternal Pillow for Your Dirt Nap.

Echoes of Death in My Mind, Tormented Souls
Silhouettes, Illusion, Permanent Intrusion
Killing You; My Choice, Killing Me; Your Voice.

Robotic Machines of War, You and Me
Your Death sealed by Fate, and My Destiny
Same Same, You and Me, I Am My Own Enemy.

The Battles Never Stop!

We own the day; "Charlie" owns the night.
You do what is right, to survive a firefight.
They are farmers by day and VC at night,
It's kill or be killed, in war there's no choice.

Training and instruction, 'Death and Destruction,'
Roller coaster, emotional distress, burnout, depressed.
It's not knowing when, the 'incoming' is coming in,
That increases anxiety, preventing your sobriety.

Blisters, heat, torrential rain, crotch rot, red muddy terrain
We're counting days to go home, we're all afraid of dying.
I gotta get outta this place, war destroys the human race.
'Nam is such a beautiful place; it's a shame, such a waste.

Once just a boy, no tan; now a spent, aging old man,
Killing fields on day 364, at last the end of my tour.
For me the war is over, yet the battles never stop,
I left Vietnam with PTSD, Vietnam has never left me.

Sand Soldiers –
A Tribute to the Gulf War Veterans
by Pfc. Jay E. Keck, USMC

Soldier Soldier in the sand
Thanks for caring and taking a stand
Soldier soldier in the sand
Those of us before you truly understand
Soldier soldier some things you need to know
Keep your weapon clean; keep your head down low
America's freedom you must keep
Soldier soldier dig in deep
Soldier soldier you have our backing
Something our VIETNAM VETS are still a lacking
Soldier soldier you give them hell
Just be yourself and you will do well
It's ok to weep, it's ok to cry
Soldier soldier some of you will surely DIE
Soldier soldier we know that 'WAR IS HELL'
We are here to help and make sure YOU GET WELL
Soldier soldier so far away in the sand
Better to fight there than in our homeland
Soldier soldier all red white and blue
Believe in your Mission and what you Must Do
Soldier soldier protecting OUR FLAG
Kick their BUTTS and come home and brag
Soldier soldier in the sand this POEM is for YOU
Being VIETNAM Vets seems the least we could do
Soldier soldier in GOD WE do TRUST
We will not leave you in the desert to rust
Brothers and Sisters in the sand
We thank you for Defending this land

NEVER AGAIN WILL ONE GENERATION of AMERICAN
VETERANS, ABANDON ANY of its VETERANS...

Living With Post Traumatic Stress Disorder
In dedication to all who are experiencing PTSD

A disorder called Post-Traumatic Stress,
It makes people's lives a mess.
They're plagued with anger, fear and dread,
They often wish that they were dead.
To live each day is a difficult test,
Nightmares rob them of a peaceful night's rest.
In time the stress makes their bodies break down,
And to the hospital they are bound.
To those who are afflicted, it's a fact,
This stress can cause a heart attack.
Their families are torn as they stand helplessly by,
"What can I do?" is their anguished cry.
As if physical ailments were not enough,
It's their mental torment that's really tough.
Some just can't bear it and sadly decide,
I'd be better off committing suicide.
In the meantime, though, they choose isolation,
Some try counseling and medication.
Still, for the families, there's a terrible strain,
To be shut out causes great pain.
Most just can't handle the problems so great,
And seek legal counsel to separate.
It's such a shame, such a tragedy,
That whole families become victims of **PTSD**.
Is there hope… a cure for this?
At the present time, we can only wish.
But in God's great love and mercy we'll find,
Peace and security in His due time.

Author Unknown

I Can Still Hear Their CRIES

Death and Dying, You Never Forget the Eyes
Friend or Foe, I Hear Their Cries
Military or Civilian, Adversary or Children
You Never Forget the Eyes
My Head Throbs, My Soul Is In Pain
I Hear Their Cries

The Nameless Faces, the Heads, are Always There
The Horror, the Suffering, Who Really Cares
The Absence of Hope in Their Eyes
Victims? I Hear Their Cries

For My Country I Served, Don't Weep
The Faith and the Honor I Did Keep
Painful Images in My Mind's Eye
Yes, I Hear Their Cries

Death and Dying, You're always Trying,
To just Forget the Eyes
And Drown out Their Cries
Military or Civilian, Adversary or Children
Your internal conflict, in trying to justify.
My Soul Is In Pain, My Heart Sobs,
Nightly I Cry For RELIEF…because
I Can Still Hear Their Cries…even in my sleep.

Survivor's Guilt

I was instructed to try to **re-assemble the dismembered body parts** collected in the two rows of newly arrived "bloated body bags" lying on the ground. After about 90 minutes of intense humid heat, blood, other body fluids and the smells of decay, my team had put the remains of (8) Men together as humanely as possible. It felt like trying to assemble a human puzzle, only these pieces were from fallen fellow Americans, humans, that were once full of LIFE, breathing, walking, talking, and doing the same things that I had done. Today, forty years later, I'm still constantly overwhelmed by thoughts of whether or not I put the right head with the right body parts. These recurring thoughts have forced me to live with those 'Heads' for over 40 years. Those 'HEADS,' they continue to HAUNT ME, as I relive that experience, day after day after day, 24/7.

YES, *I can still hear their cries, even in my sleep!*

Four of my high school classmates joined the military services immediately after graduation. At my suggestion, they told their recruiters that I had referred them. Because of my enlistment within the Naval Reserve unit while we were all still in school, I received a pay grade promotion and a letter of commendation. A dear friend and fellow classmate, who like me, had also achieved the rank of high school R.O.T.C. Cadet Captain in our fourth year, (Corporal Larry Martin, USMC) was killed only a few miles from my base camp.

Those two infants that died in my arms, both painfully laboring to breathe, left me feeling totally helpless. I still see their faces. I also felt helpless that day at the Chu Lai Airfield, watching a young marine, whose intestines protruded through a softball size wound; call out for his "Momma" with his last breath.

I'm plagued with tormenting thoughts and internal inquisitions of why I have lived and others didn't. Unable to justify my earthy existence, I began to self-medicate myself with alcohol and drugs, which would only dilute and temporally subdue my demons of death. I can't seem to forgive myself, neither can I rationalize absolution, nor remove my aching soul from the depths of self-blame. Recurring nightmares, flashbacks, and facial intrusions of the dead certainly don't help the healing process either. *I can still hear their cries, even in my sleep.*

County law enforcement agents seemingly patrol by air twenty four hours a day, seven days a week, circling and hovering in '*choppers*' directly overhead. I am bothered by the sounds of helicopters, and those low flying spotter planes which are constant reminders of Vietnam. Just like back in 'The Nam,' I can hear them approaching from miles away. Almost all sudden and startling loud noises will instigate an immediate elevated heart rate and several moments of tense uneasy feelings day or night.

The complete abstinence of alcohol and illegal drugs, combined with individual psychotherapy, group counseling, time and medication have permitted me the façade of stability. Daily prayers, plus my belief in the almighty creator, who gives and sustains all life, have given me enduring faith, which allows me to cope with everyday life. I know that it is only by the grace of God that I am still here, I know not why, nor do I know the depth of my earthly mission. I wrestle with this lonesome burden known as "Survivor's Guilt" daily, and every day I ask myself, "Why am I here?" and "Why did I live?" Only God knows. Perhaps the penning of these poems is a part of that mission, and I give thanks daily for life itself, as well as the multitude of blessings that the Creator has bestowed upon me. I know that YOU, Dear Lord, hath smiled on me, I pray that I am worthy. The Love of God, and my totally supportive wife Jessica, permits me to thrive and survive. Thank You, Dear Lord. Thank you for allowing me to see another day.

The Valley of Despair, aka PTSD

During one of my depressing low ebb tide moments I wrote: "Death is my best buddy, my constant companion, my thoughts, the memories, the flashbacks. As I dwell in the recesses of the valley of despair, by choice, I have slumbered in the dark caverns of depression, hiding, withdrawn from reality, seeking pity and reparations because I had internalized that the world owed me something. Steeped in alcohol and drugs and confined within my self-induced, self-fulfilling prophetic hellish condition and saturated with a constant illusion of hopelessness, I sought to end the anguish, the frustration, the mental torment. My thoughts were focused on freeing my suffering tormented soul by taking own life. Why? Because I felt that my wretched life had no positive direction, no meaning or purpose. So I kissed steel, and suckled on a cold blue tube, waiting, anticipating and preparing to welcome the unforgiving flaming messengers of death. My gun barrel became a lollipop without a sugar coating or a fruit flavored topping; it was however, just an obedient servant poised to release its power and deadly force. The trigger reluctantly maneuvered with resistance as I anticipated the explosive deadly projectile invading my body, searing and burning as it traveled upward to my brain. Again, 'Time Stood Still' as my life flashed by and replayed within my mind. My mind was weak, my spirit was muddled, my odor challenged body was soaked with alcohol and perspiration, my hands began to shake, causing the gun barrel to irritate my tongue, forcing me to gag. As I withdrew the four inch 357 Colt Python revolver from my mouth, my tongue managed to 'French' the barrel tip momentarily as it exited. My pounding heart attempted to escape from its imprisoned cage, and the ringing in my ears became almost deafening. So I slowly repositioned that bitter-tasting 357, placing it directly under my chin and angled backwards for maximum penetration and effectiveness. Agonizing thoughts intruded my consciousness as I blinked my moistened eyes in an effort to continue without succumbing to my fear. Knowing that some gun shot head wounds liquefy the contact area into chunks and/or a bloody, flakey, oatmeal type paste, I didn't want to think too long about pulling that trigger. So I smiled, as I had visions of others cleaning up the chunks of my brain and the massive pool of jellied congealed blood." **HA – HA HA –HA aaah.** How morbid is that? I snickered. My head throbbed, my soul was in pain. Then I bowed my head and called out for help.

A Plea from the Valley

O my God, I seek refuse in you Father
Against Satin the devil, spawn of evil.
O Lord of the worlds, I call unto thee
For guidance and discerning wisdom.

Father protect me from harm, as only
You can, from the enemy within & without.
Devine Creator; please grant unto me health,
Peace of mind, happiness and prosperity.

Most Merciful, Most Beneficent God, Lord
Bless me with enduring strength as I struggle
To find my way back to sanity and salvation
Within All your Books, and from Geneses to Revelation.
Thank You, Thank you Lord for giving me one more day. . .

Concluding Narrative

Gang Bangers that wage war within our communities, ('the hood'), to me, are like young children playing nursery games, compared to **dancing with death in Vietnam.** In the hood you 'throw down' over your 'street rep' (credibility), 'territorial turf pride' of (your residential area), 'tag's' (individual or group identifiers), and clothing 'colors,' mainly via those cowardly 'drive by's' in vehicles. What if those 'gangster wanna-be' types had to sit back to back with a partner all night long, one sleeps and the other watches? Or what if they had to track their enemy for miles on foot, for days at a time? Try traveling at a nonstop pace, while hacking through thick, five to eight feet high elephant grass with machetes. How brave would they be? Envision laying flat on your stomach all night in one place, unable to move, talk, or smoke, as different types of biting insects, rodents, and snakes seek to drain your warm blood. At daybreak you see flattened grass trails where your enemy had laid all night, just inches away from you. During the night they (your enemy), stealthy approached your ambush set up area, crawling inch by inch, in anticipation of someone from your patrol giving their exact position away. They now had choices that you knew nothing about—open fire on you at a point-blank range, reverse the direction of your own booby traps which you would inevitably accidentally detonate in the morning, or quietly slit a few throats and slither away before sunrise. What if you were searching for an elusive small sized band of ruthless marauders, who had pillaged nearby villages for food, kidnapped fresh young recruits, raped and killed women, children, and the elderly? Suddenly your group finds out that they are greatly outnumbered, and this small unit is actually ten times larger than expected. You are caught in the midst of a cleverly devised trap. Now you're the hunted ones, running on foot, for your life and being chased (over the river and through the woods [jungles]) in humid 100 degree-plus temperatures. Anyone can point a gun out of moving vehicle; however, in real combat situations, life and death is truly a 24 hour-7 day a week hell, a living nightmare. Black, brown, white, or yellow, you depend on each other, for life.

The Opinions and views expressed within are mine solely, and are not reflective of any particular group, class or cross section of society; they evolved from my life experiences as youth; a man-child and an aging veteran. However, every returning combat veteran has a *complex mixture of internal conflicts raging within*, a series of '*mini wars*'. Historically, all of our returning U.S. combat veterans had weeks, even months to '*decompress*' from the battlefield before being returned to their home dinner table. Except Vietnam, we broke the mold, going from "the Nam" back to "the Hood" in less than 48 hrs. We didn't have time to mourn, reflect, be debriefed or adjust to being back home. We trickled back home and became a shock to an unsuspecting society, who treated us like an unwanted, uninvited relative. America, land that I love, reluctantly tolerated its returning warriors.

Remember that we, the United States Military Veteran, are the physical extensions of your Political Cerebral Ideologies. **So Please consider the real victims of war, the dead and those who must live with Death!** I repeat, Gang Wars in the 'hood' are like playing nursery games compared to <u>dancing with death in Vietnam</u>.

In my novel, "**<u>Dancing with Death-All gave some, Some gave ALL</u>**", *my story is revealed in much greater detail*, however, **I didn't tell it ALL, I couldn't.**

My guilt ridden story, however, is just one of hundreds of thousands yet to be told. There are many tales of woe and tiny segments of the lives of thousands upon thousands of battle tested combatants **that <u>will never be told</u>.** *Partly because some of us may still be caring the burdens of survivors guilt, while others are too ashamed of their past deeds.* However, the facts of the business are: *most of us have locked those traumatic events deep within the recesses of our minds for safe-keeping, and well-being,* OUR OWN.

With the blessings of Our Creator, Lord and Master, I shall overcome and control my inner passions. Even though the war is over, the Battles never stop. Yes, for all of us Vets, <u>the war is over, but the PTSD battles never stop</u>!!!

They NEVER STOP for me, because...
I CAN STILL HEAR THEIR CRIES---Even In My Sleep.
E. Everett McFall **USMC "Corpsman" (medic)**

A Message to the Reader:

As You Read, You Walked In My Shoes,
Are You Shocked, Sadden, or Feeling Blue?
I Wanted to Enlighten and Educate You,
On PTSD and What We Go Through.
Did You Feel The Anguish, The Pain?
Then My Goals Were Attained,
Thank You and May God Bless You.

E. Everett McFall
Class of Vietnam 1966-67
PTSD and Purple Heart Recipient
"In Country 12 months, in Therapy ever since"

Tips For Vets and the Families Who Are Managing Stress

If you are a Combat Veteran, or if you know someone that is a Combat Veteran, seek professional help for depression, roller coaster mood swings, uncontrollable anger, flashbacks and nightmares, and any existing medical problems now!!! Call your local Veterans Administration Medical Facility and or your nearest Vet Center to talk about your feelings and reactions. You need HELP NOW!

Stress is a silent *Killer* that can also cause Hypertension, Stroke, Severe Medical Conditions and Permanent Loss of Sight. Stress can increase anger and those feelings of helplessness. You are not alone; there are tens of thousands of other Vets going through or have experienced the same feelings, so reach out to them through a VA center or a National Service Organization if you feel overwhelmed. You don't have to live in silence, suffering with GUILT, HELPLESSNESS, ANGER and DEPRESSION!

You have PTSD, it's not contagious and you are not crazy. The war was beyond your control. HELP is available right now, for you and your family. It's free and totally confidential with personalized individual and group sessions. You are not "The ONLY ONE GOING THROUGH THIS". You SURVIVED; you are alive, **Welcome Home.**

Here are some important things that you can do to help your advocate present your claim effectively.

- Give the advocate a copy of your discharge papers **(DD214).**
- Give your advocate **copies of any service medical or private medical records you have.**
- Give your advocate **copies of any service records you may have.**
- **Make a list of all of your dependants** *(including children in college)* and have *copies of their birth certificates, and* *marriage***(s)** *certificate***(s).**
- Give your advocate a written account of *anything that happened to you in service that you think might have caused a current disability.*
- Give your advocate a *written history* of your *symptoms and treatment* for *any disability that you think might be connected to your military service.*
- Have a *written history* of the *people who have observed your symptoms since your separation* from the military, how and where can these people be contacted.
- Tell your advocate *if you have applied for, or received,* any *other disability benefits such as Social Security disability payments.*
- Provide a *full account of all of your income and assets* (**net worth**) to help your advocate consider *your possible entitlement to pension.*

KEEP copies of everything that you receive from the VA. GIVE a copy to your advocate. KEEP the ORIGINAL, and copies of everything that you give to your advocate. Start collecting the documentation that you need now, don't wait until you see an advocate. These organizations usually have an office and 'service representatives' located in the same building of the nearest VA Regional Office. Be Patient and be prepared to wait for responses, it takes time for paperwork to flow through the official channels of the 'Governmental' system.

Veterans Resource Guide and Directory

You will need a certified copy of your discharge summary. To obtain a copy of your DD214, go to: www.archives.gov or call 866-272-6272

You can also contact your own state Dept. of Veterans Affairs for a copy of your DD214

U.S. Department of Veterans Affairs
www.va.gov
VA Benefits   800-827-1000
VA Health Care Benefits   877-222-8387
> Request a copy of 'Federal Benefits for Veterans & Dependents.' There are no time limits or deadline for applying for disability payments.

Gulf War/Agent Orange Help Line	**800-749-8387**
National Gulf War Resource Center	**800-882-1316, x 162**
Telecommunication Device for Deaf (TDD)	**800-820-4833**
Social Security administration www.ssa.gov	**800-772-1213**

There are numerous veterans' organizations that assist veterans. Some serve as claims representatives as well. If you are considering whether you should or even if you need to file a claim for compensation or pension, we suggest that you consult with a service representative of one of the following national service organizations.

National Service Organizations:

American Legion
700 No. Pennsylvania St.
PO Box 1055
Indianapolis, IN 46206
317-630-1200
www.legion.org

American Vets (Amvets)
4647 Forbes Boulevard
Lanham, MD 20706
301-726-8387
www.amvets.org

Disabled American Veterans
National Headquarters
3725 Alexandria Pike
Cold Spring, KY 41076
859-441-7300
www.dav.org

Veterans of Foreign Wars
National Headquarters
406 W. 34th Street
Kansas City, MO 64111
816-756-3390
www.vfw.org

Vietnam Veterans of America
8605 Cameron Street, Suite 400
Silver Springs, MD 20910
1-800-VVA-1316
www.vva.org

OTHER RESOURCES
Al-Anon Family Group Headquarters
800-344-2666
www.al-anon.alateen.org

Alcoholics Anonymous
212-870-3400
www.alcoholics-anonymous.org
Anxiety Disorders Association of America
11900 Parklawn Drive, Suite 100
Rockville, MD 20852
301-231-9350
www.adaa.org

International Society for Traumatic Stress Studies
60 Revere Drive, Suite 500
Northbrook, IL 60062
847-480-9028
www.istss.org

Military Order of the Purple Heart
National Headquarters
5413-B Backlick Rd.
Springfield, VA, 22151
888-668-1656
www.purpleheart.org

National Center for Post Traumatic Stress Disorder
VA Medical Center (116 D)
White River Junction, VT 05009
802-296-5132
www.ncptsd.org/
www.ncptsd.org/faq.html?
www.ncptsd.org/treatment/index.html?

National Mental Health Consumer
Self-Help Clearinghouse
1211 Chestnut St. 11th floor
Philadelphia, PA 19101
800-688-4226
www.mentalhelp.net

Substance Abuse and Mental Health Services Administration
800-622-HELP
www.samhsa.gov
www.findtreatment.samhsa.gov

Go to: http://my.webmd.com/encyclopedia/article/2950.1505
                                                    /2950.1509
                                                    /2950.1508
                                                    /2950.1507
                                                    /2950.1506

Go to: www.popasmoke.com/vietnam-war-facts.html

Suggested Reading Sources:

"Survivor Guilt, A Self-Help Guide"
 by   Aphrodite Matsakis

"Trauma & Recovery: The Aftermath of Violence-from Domestic Abuse to Political Terror"
 by   Judith Lewis Herman

"Veterans & Families Guide to Recovering From PTSD"
 By   Stephanie L. Lanham   exclusively distributed by:
 Purple Heart Service Foundation, P.O. Box 49
 Annandale, VA 22003
  www.purpleheart.org/service.htm

 "The Things They Carried"
 By Tim O' Brien

"Chickenhawk"
 By Robert Mason

"Post Traumatic Stress Disorder: A Handbook for Clinicians"
 Edited by Tom Williams
 Published by the Disabled American Veterans

Vietnam War Photo Book--
Poems From The Bogeyman
Vietnam Photo DVD

> Contact: Jay E. Keck USMC
> P.O. Box 71
> Wolcottville, IN 46795
> j.keck@mchsi.com

"Firebase Ripcord", a Medics Story
> By Martin J. Glennon, U.S. Army
> 219 –759 – 2022

"Vietnam- The Other Side of Glory"
> By William R. Kimball

"Dancing With Death, All Gave Some-Some Gave All"
> By E. Everett McFall /USMC Medic
> (Release date still pending-2008)
> P.O. Box 11557
> Merrillville, IN 46411

You should watch with caution:

Oliver Stone's	- **"Platoon"**
Stanley Kubrick's	- **"Full Metal Jacket"**
Mel Gibson's	- **"We Were Soldier's"**
Jamie Fox's	- **"Jarhead"**

You have just taken a Journey into my Combat PTSD…Simper Fi !!!

Reviews

"I Can Still Hear Their Cries, Even in My Sleep by E. Everett McFall is an outstanding portrayal of the deep inner feelings about war and its mental and physical consequences, which resulted in his Post Traumatic Stress Disorder (PTSD).

The author's words are powerful and absorbing as he describes his despair in dealing with the realities of war and the lifelong healing process which he is experiencing. It gives the novice a much better understanding of PTSD and its effects on the mind and body.

Mr. McFall expresses his feelings with vivid verbal pictures enabling everyone to see though his eyes. This is a book which should be read by all."

Samuel W. Hurley, USAF, WWII

"E. Everett McFall's collection 'I Can Still Hear Their Cries', is a cathartic work that takes a reader into the torment and pain of a Vietnam War veteran who, through poetry and prose, provides a reader with a shocking sensory insight into life as a Marine Medic and a surviving veteran. His poetry is vivid, visual, honest, compelling and painful. McFall, I commend you for your candid openness, your vulnerability and capacity to reach others who are too often overlooked. We believe that this work could provide support for ALL veterans and their families."

Dr. Regina V. Jones, Professor, Indiana
University Northwest, Dept. of Minority Studies

"In his collection of work entitled "I Can Still Hear Their Cries, Even in My Sleep" the author E. Everett McFall, a Purple Heart recipient, discusses his experiences with Post Traumatic Stress Disorder through his poetry. He details the causes of the "scars" in his mind, such as memories of the "eyes of death and dying" and "whistling sounds of incoming mortars." In one narrative, McFall describes PTSD as a "valley of despair" and reflects upon the mental anguish and torment.

Throughout his poetry he describes the painful images of the Vietnam War and the suffering experienced by everyone involved as well as camaraderie's created during the war. He includes tips for veterans and their families on coping with stress and depression. This book also contains a veteran's resource guide and directory of National Service Organizations as well as recommended reading materials."

Jean Wahlborg, Editorial Coordinator

"A dynamic, heart wrenching and emotionally draining book. It that educates, shocks, inspires and informs the non-warrior and the combatant. He invites his students to emotionally participate in an indictment of war; some will regrettably relive the trauma."

Elder Dr. Dale Cudjoe, Pastor, CTCOC (Holiness) U.S.A., Northern Diocese

"This was truly an honor to read this manuscript, which expresses the most vivid picture of a tough and challenging time in your life. I was captivated with the sincerity and the creative way you expressed yourself while depicting a horrible time and situation. I have watched movies, listened to others speak, and read several writings from those who shared war related experiences, but never has anyone successfully moved me the way this book has done. I just couldn't stop reading it. We pray for your continued internal healing through the power of Jesus, our Lord and Savior."

Elder Don C. Williams, Associate Minister, Church of Christ (Holiness) USA Northern Diocese.

"I was impressed by this compilation of poems depicting the Vietnam War. It was an easy read, *compelling and captivating* to the point that you can't put it down until you've turned the last page. A "*MUST READ*" for the families of Veterans of any war, who must deal with the residual after affects of war on their loved ones."

Earmon Irons, Deacon / Spiritual Advisor

"This author has a chilling affect on readers with his highly charged and emotional use of words. "I Can Still Hear Their Cries, Even in My Sleep" is a befitting title. He is fresh, expressive, vivid, and thought provoking. He challenges you to close your eyes as you visually navigate this 'passage into the depths of reality of war' and his journey into PTSD."

Sherry Knox, Clinical Social Worker

"A powerful, poetic journal that is insightful, revealing, timely and therapeutic. Fact a business, we are extremely proud of our adopted son, 'Everett', and we pray that God will continue blessing him."

"Mom & Pop"
Ida and PFC Hubert Jackson, US Army WWII

About the Author:

Born and raised in mid-western Chicago, a product of a religious, hard working middle class family. Borderline average academically, he set out to become a Medical Doctor in order to fulfill a promise to his grandmother, Mrs Margaret "Margie" Holiday. After a planned initial tour in the United States Navy as a medical corpsman, E. Everett was to enroll in college and medical school under a military funded program. His life's dream of being a Naval Doctor was de-railed and side-tracked during his 364 days in the Republic of Vietnam from 1966 to 1967.

As a U.S. Marine Corps Field Medical Corpsman he served with pride and distinction, receiving a field promotion while 'in country', and he participated in 11 major offensive combat operations in 1967;

Operation Cleveland	24 Jan	--	Operation Independence	01 Feb
Operation Stone	12 Feb	--	Operation Pulaski	24 Feb
Operation Yuba	10 Mar	--	Operation Big Horn	05 Apr
Operation Shawnee	24 Apr	--	Operation Chacktaw	22 May
Operation Freemont	10 Jun	--	Operation Granite	26 Oct
Operation Neosho	01 Nov	--	Departed Vietnam	07 Nov

A mortar barrage counter attack by the Viet Cong Insurgent Forces during Operation Shawnee, resulted in several men from his unit being wounded on 29 April 1967, including E. Everett. His good and honorable service has earned him: The Purple Heart, The Presidential Unit Citation, The Nation Defense Service Metal, The Viet Nam Service Metal with Bronze Star, The Viet Nam Campaign Metal with Device & FMF Combat Insignia...and the gratitude of those who served with him.

After 40 years, over 44 jobs, three failed marriages, and five years of psychological therapy, E. Everett McFall, is now a full time student at the Indiana University Northwest, and is now on the path of healing and reconciliation with his family and *his personal inner demons.* When he speaks of them he says,

"I can still hear their cries, even in my sleep"…

To contact authors, email: info@icanstilltheircries.com

JEM Marketing Inc.

Jessica and Ernest McFall, will personalize an autographed copy of "UnSelfish Love" with the name of your choice. Clearly Print the name in Bold BLOCK letters on a sheet of paper with your Name, Address, Tel # and Email add. Enclose $ 11.95 Check or Money Order to:

Jessica McFall
c/o Unselfish Love
P.O. Box 11557
Merrillville, IN 46411
Please allow 4 to 6 weeks for processing and shipping.

Non autographed copies can be purchased online at:
http://www.amazon.com Then enter authors name or the title
(Proceeds have been assigned to charity.)

Ernest McFall, will personalize an autographed copy of "I Can Still Hear Their Cries, Even In My Sleep" with the name of your choice. Clearly print the name in Bold BLOCK letters on a sheet of paper with your Name, Address, Tel # and Email add.
Enclose $ 13.95 Check or Money Order to:

Jessica McFall
c/o CRIES
P.O. Box 11557
Merrillville, IN 46411
Please allow 4 to 6 weeks for processing and shipping.
Non autographed copies can be purchased online at:
http://www.amazon.com   or
http://www.outskirtspress.com/icanstilltheircries.

Be sure to visit these sites:

Visit our blog at: http://eeverettmcfall.blogspot.com
we welcome your comments and reviews.

For Brazilian Acai Health Drink
www.MyJemMarketing.Net

For Healthy Lifestyle Information-
www.MyJemarketing.com

For Legal Digital Downloads-
www.MyDigitalMusicSite.Com

For Editing & Proofreading-
mcvnolan@yahoo.com

LaVergne, TN USA
27 April 2010
180754LV00004B/68/A